GYPROCK,

BREAKING DANGEROUS HABITS

AuthorHouse™
1663 Liberty Drive
Bloomington, IN 47403
www.authorhouse.com
Phone: 833-262-8899

This book is printed on acid-free paper.

ISBN: 979-8-8230-1215-7 (sc)
ISBN: 979-8-8230-1216-4 (e)

Print information available on the last page.

Published by AuthorHouse 07/28/2023

authorHOUSE®

GYPROCK,
BREAKING DANGEROUS HABITS

BRIAN ECHENBERG

DELAYING TECHNIQUE

The important and frightening thing was the momentum. When I would start to break things, the more I broke, the more I would break. Also, the more things I would fix, the less likely I would go back to banging and breaking things. At the time of this writing, I don't break much, but I bet I would panic if I started again. When the walls were new, I'd feel good again, even if they wouldn't look good to others. A wall that was intact and not dented—would often hit the Gyprock with my hand and make a dent—and had wet or dry plaster but no paint or sanding made me feel proud. Most people take for granted a painted, intact, "perfect" wall, but I don't. Here on Beaconsfield, a place where I broke things at the beginning but never to the extent I did when I was Richmond, I have plywood walls in some places and double Gyprock in the main bathroom. I even have a glass wall in that bathroom, something completely unthinkable in the past. I think it's neat to have that glass wall. It's a victory and a big accomplishment.

Another thing I did that was very destructive was break sinks, pipes, and bathroom mirrors. Bathrooms were potentially dangerous. There would be a lot of breakable items. One time, I went to a well-known bar and yanked out the pipes and fixture holding the urinal to the wall in the public bathroom. The metal pipe came loose, and water started pouring from the wall. I panicked and, of course, was all wet. I quickly exited the bathroom with nobody seeing me, no witnesses. I went back to my table—actually, it was kind of a counter or bar—and acted like I knew nothing about what was going on, but I was all wet. A waiter was watching me and wondering why I was wet. People were running through the bar yelling that there was two feet of water in the bathroom. Police came, along with fire trucks. People were saying there was a flood.

Glass has always been my nemesis—windows, light fixtures, drinking glasses, windshields. When I went into a room, I used to avoid walking near the windows because, if I did, I would have to hit them or at least touch them. In my apartments, I would sleep in the center of the room, far from where I would hit the windows.

I would always "test" glass. If I didn't hit the glass, I felt I had to push it to see how far I could go without breaking it. It was a habit. Glass was always a problem for me. When I would finally bust the window, it was actually horrifying. I was trying to see how much the glass would give, but I didn't want it to break. The point was just to get the feeling of chance or risk to satisfy me. When the glass of the window broke, like Gyprock, I felt I had to fix it or have it fixed as soon as possible. I would only do these things with my right hand and, as a consequence, only have scars on that hand. I've had a lot of stitches there and also scars and damage to my right leg and foot from kicking things, especially walls.

One time at Ogilvy's I tried to kick something in the bathroom, but my shin hit the sink hard. I'm sure I broke a bone. My leg was very swollen. Another time, on Decarie, I kicked the wall very high, and my foot broke the thick plaster. I got a bad cut in my foot just above the heel. I went to the hospital, and they tried to get all the pieces of plaster out of the cut. Several stitches were put in. When I came home to my basement apartment, I seemed to be satisfied in a way and felt calm. I watched TV and ordered chicken. Funny—but when I'd finally cut or hurt myself, I'd feel satiated.

On Decarie, the walls were hard and thick; there was heavy plaster, in both the apartments and the hallways. One thing that was hard for me to do was replace the long florescent bulbs in the hallways. Carrying the bulb to the fixture was difficult because I felt I had to knock the bulb almost hard enough to break it but not quite. It wasn't a matter of just hitting the glass but, rather, of pushing it. One time in the back alley behind Decarie, I was walking and was nervous. I saw in the garbage a box of florescent bulbs. These kind would explode, not break, when you broke them, and I kicked the box. They all exploded and made a huge mess. A man came out to the back loading dock and just looked at me.

Even past my worst time, on Beaconsfield, I broke lots of windows. I broke two out of three panels of glass in the bay window—the big center one and one of the sides. To this day, that side window is bent. Thermal glass, too, I broke. Outside of the bathroom in the hall there was a big thermal pane that I broke at least twice.

When I had my old front and side doors with small panes of glass inserted, I must have broken them ten times. These panes were not thick. I would hit them, not punch them, to see how hard I could hit without them breaking. The only time I would leave them alone was right after they were fixed. Then I seemed to want to keep them intact, but pretty soon the novelty of the repaired glass wore off. The time immediately following the repair was my favorite time. The time right after busting one window or two was the most dangerous. I would hit other windows harder in a panic after, and it would be hard to stop.

Panic and precedence were the enemies. If I could stop for a little while, I could build on that and try to fix the damage instead of breaking more things. But definitely it was a habit and a matter of momentum. I would usually feel better at one point and build on that. But I wouldn't waste any time and would be in a rush to take stock of the damage and start to fix things. For example, if I broke the kind of window I could remove and bring to glass experts, I would. Then I'd go on to the next repair. Many times just cleaning the mess would be enough to get me started to "come back" or "bounce back." If I broke the wall, I would vacuum or sweep up and feel better. I would start the renewal process.

You have to understand that damage is very hard to stop once it's underway. I had to break the feeling of despair and panic the series of breaking things would cause. One time on Beaconsfield, I kicked my bedroom door and the closet doors. As I got less controlled and felt worse, I kicked them harder and harder.

If I could lie down peacefully for just ten minutes, I would have success. But if I lay down in bed and felt uneasy, I would get up and start the damage again. The best thing was to take a nap for one or two hours. It was panic and fear and, more than anything, the failure to control myself. But now I know it wasn't my fault. It was like walking down Decarie to Murray's—almost impossible sometimes. It's hard to explain to someone who doesn't know about severe obsessive-compulsive behavior.

On Decarie, the more things I would touch and knock, the more I would be worked into a state where I had less and less control. It became unbearable; it was the worst I felt about myself. And the crazier I felt, the more people would stare at me. Anybody, I guess, would stare at someone yelling and retracing his steps while trying to cross the street and doing it over and over maybe ten times. In my head, I was almost completely oblivious to reality. It was awful. The Anafranil medication would help this when the OCD was at its worst. But if I could manage to reach Murray's a bit intact mentally, I might settle down. You could be sure, though, I would be in no hurry to get back on the street again.

Aprepot was a gift shop next to Murray's, and I would try to buy things, but many of the things were breakable. So in my attempt to be normal and have nice things, I would buy a lot. I wanted to challenge myself with glasses and dishes and anything breakable. I wanted to see how long I could keep them in my apartment. I would buy nice furniture that I would almost, for sure, break and kick. But I felt good with a new bedroom furniture set, even if the walls were demolished. It felt good to have nice things in my apartment.

It was always a balance between breaking things and recovering. It was like a war, with attacks and counterattacks—the attacks being damage and the counterattacks being fixing and feeling better.

I used Raymond to fix the walls. He was a friend and a good worker. But there came a point where he didn't feel right being part of the cycle. He said, "I can't do this anymore," that it wasn't good. He felt bad fixing some hole or whole wall and then coming back and repairing the exact same wall again two days later. Over the weekends when he wouldn't work, he would come back on the Monday and say, "This weekend you really went to town." I paid him well, but I think he felt bad about me throwing my money away.

Money was the one weapon in the war I had on my side. I could always afford to fix things and, moreover, live in a place where I could do what I did and make that much noise. On Decarie, there was a young man upstairs from the office who—before I started going into rages—would go into almost the same type of rages. He would yell and bang and kick things. And I would feel sorry for him. Little did I know, in the same building years later, I would be the "crazy one."

Raymond used to live in apartment 6 in my father's office apartment. Later on, when he moved out was when I needed him most. I know he felt sorry for me. But having money to live in a building my father owned was my salvation. In another building, I would have been kicked out and have ended up either in jail or a hospital.

Also on Richmond, I owned my town house. But I did have to answer to people, as there were pissed-off neighbors. One time, the developer who owned a part of the building came there to talk to me. At that time, I was very belligerent and used to get into fights because of my fear, rages, and anger. But he wasn't afraid of me like many people. I told Donald if he came up the stairs again to my unit, I would kick him downstairs.

In Richmond, I had friends who used to visit me. Many times it involved music or jamming. Morrie who passed away, would come. And so would Kenny. I can only imagine what they thought of my living quarters. I would calm down when I was busy and would become occupied with what I was doing—like when I was playing music. I didn't break things when I had a visitor.

But one time, Beverly came to my place and said I should get help. I broke a nice drum machine. "You could have given it to me instead of breaking it," Kenny said.

He was a close friend, and we would jam, although he wasn't that good. I can only imagine what he thought of my situation.

Morrie used to come to my basement apartment on Decarie. We would go for Chinese food at night because he would take a nap and get up very late. But he always wanted to sit apart from the other customers because of the noise I would make. If he hadn't passed away, he would have made a good witness to testify about my predicament. He called my apartment "Berlin 1945".

Also on Decarie, my Uncle Joe would call me on Sundays and try to help me. He was that kind of guy—extremely benevolent and thought of everyone else but himself. He called my making noise and yelling "hiccups." That was about the time my father died, and I took a real turn for the worst.

Right from the start, Beaconsfield was safer, more secure, and homier because I lived in a self-contained house. The only problems I had were with my East Indian neighbors. The father attacked me, and they were very hostile with me. Living next to them was very uncomfortable. But besides that, I didn't get any complaints.

Decarie was terrible. But Richmond might have been the worst and potentially the most dangerous, as I shared the building with others. I lived there for maybe nine months. Although the place was new and nice, the walls were very thin. Noise and damage were constant concerns. There was little left of the walls after a while. All the doors were missing because doors were one of the first things I would kick, and the doors at Richmond were hollow and very breakable. The construction of the town house was not made for someone with my issues. So, I broke all but the front door of the town house and made a lot of noise doing it. In addition, all the kitchen cupboard doors were soon broken and missing.

Ronnie came over to Richmond to jam and asked why there were no doors. I don't know what I said. Someone else remarked that the town house must not be finished, as the repaired walls were bare, with just plaster and no paint. There wasn't anything I could say.

As far as resilience went concerning the damage, it was at a low point. It seemed like the whole time I was there—a period of months—I was just breaking things. I would still go to Murray's and the office, although my father was gone by 1982. I still considered Murray's as my retreat. It would calm me down and perk me up.

In the town house, as opposed to my house on Beaconsfield, there weren't many, or really any, periods of calm. Breaking things was pretty much constant. And although I ordered barbecue chicken, I didn't have much relief. The more I broke, the more agitated I got. And I definitely never felt secure, as I wasn't alone in the building. I think there were varying degrees of damage. And probably, when I had company, I would take a "break" and would have my mind more occupied on other things. But I still "loved" going to Murray's and enjoyed meeting people there.

It might have been a bit better than Cranbrooke, where I had no privacy or security and was a man of rituals. On Cranbrooke, I was threatened seriously with violence by my crazy neighbor next to me. He was old but big and scary. He threatened me. And when I kicked the walls and furniture at night he would come after me. My father alive then, so it was before 1982. My neighbor said either he would kill me, or I would have to kill him. He smashed my side car window and chased me with a gun—possibly a fake one. He terrorized me.

During this time, I got some relief by playing in Lachute and Brownsburg in a country band, me playing guitar. I would drive out there in my Datsun B-210 but would have issues with the bass player. He also terrorized me a bit, but I didn't have to live next to him. My resilience was still there at these times, but there were fewer bouts of calm and almost no relaxation. I was not secure at all in my living quarters, and I didn't have a safe haven!

The key to stop breaking things was to resist the urge or not to think about it. If I was lying in bed and I got the feeling that I wanted to kick or hit something, I would lose the battle. The trick would be to avoid the feeling, which would translate to an itch almost, and it would only be satiated by kicking or hitting. Many times, I would feel something of an urge or itch to kick something, but I could sublimate it by kicking the floor. Still, I had to get relief by kicking something. This urge would feed off itself, and before I knew it, something would be broken. A nap or being exhausted mentally and going to sleep was good. When I was asleep, I wouldn't damage anything. And I would wake up in a new frame of mind or refreshed.

Summer and heat made it worse. Some air-conditioner upstairs was a salvation. Hot weather, and people getting irritated as a result, was much worse for me and my rituals. But taking a nap in a cool room would be great.

On Decarie, I lived part of the time in the apartment in the basement and part of the time in apartment 6 on the first floor. The basement was dark and cool, good for sleeping, which was a break for me. In the basement, I would cover the bedroom window and sleep into the afternoon and wake up at 2:00 p.m. But sleeping so late, I woke up anxious and nervous. I would try to make my way to Murray's as best I could and get there with as little ritual as possible.

By the time I walked back to 4620 Decarie in fall or winter, it was already dark. And I would feel bad that I'd missed all the light.

In apartment 6,in summer, it would get hot, and the apartment was dirty and drab. It wasn't the type of home I had been brought up in, and I missed Alpine. Those were the two apartments at 4620 I lived in, but I also lived down the street (south) in the Frank Quinn Bldg. A neighbor who lived directly above me couldn't stand my noise and asked if (or assumed) I was epileptic. He said my front door wouldn't stop him if he stayed. I was afraid of people or neighbors and thought I would drive someone to bodily harm.

But it's funny. Once again, Murray's was my relief. Cindy, the waitress, was very nice to me. I know she liked me. We ended up selling her the 1976 Chevy Nova, and she later worked at the Vielle Kitzbuel. Some people were freaked out by my behavior, but not her. At that time, I would yell a very distinct, very loud, "Hey." It would awaken the attention of all around, but Cindy overlooked it. I would sometimes be very nervous at Murrays and yell and definitely hit the table hard so the silverware and utensils would make a rattling that was satisfying to me. Other times, when fewer people were there, not at a meal time, I felt calmer and more relaxed. But I swore also. And with the noise of the table and the yelling, people were shocked. I sat at the table usually, and people at my table would quickly change their seats—aside from Eddy, that is. Eddy was a weird guy I would sit with and talk to, who had a big crush on Cindy. He was the kind of guy I wouldn't have much to do with if I was feeling or acting normal.

One time not that long ago actually, I went into the CIBC bank on Somerled. I was nervous and felt like banging something. I felt like that because things weren't responding as quickly as I would have liked them to. For example, I was trying to use my bank card to open the front door, but it wasn't happening right away. So, I used the bank machine and was getting more and more frustrated—until I started banging on the instant teller. Then on the way out of the bank, after I'd worked myself into a state, I started punching the front inside glass door. It shattered, and I cut myself.

I quickly walked away bleeding, and a woman on the street said, "Did you just break that window?"

I just walked on. It was like the time on Decarie, when I kicked the carpet store front glass door and smashed it. Luckily that time, there was no one around to be a witness. In the bank incident, I might have been accused or suspected of trying to rob it or in the case of the carpet store, trying to break in. But I think, more likely, I would have been taken to the hospital for a psychiatric examination. Anyone who knew me would know I had money and was not trying to rob a place. One time, also on the way to Murray's, I was having a particularly hard time with my rituals. They were driving me crazy, and I was losing control. I went downstairs to the bathroom and kicked or hit the sink, and water came out. Even though no one saw me, I knew they suspected me. It was a bit like the country ban years later but not as bad.

Usually when I broke something in public, it was due to rituals or to my anxiety and tics driving me to distraction. I would never do it for the fun of it or consciously. I would go into a kind of trance, separated from the reality of the situation. I would say I wasn't in my right mind. I would also be shocked by the deed and would act normal or calm afterward, as if the incident had brought me back to reality. I would be jarred and wouldn't break more at that time, unlike the damage I would do in the places where I lived. In public, I would be scared. It would be like walking through a minefield. Danger was everywhere. I wasn't safe until I got to where I was heading. Usually, I only felt a bit safe when I was finally home or at Murray's—safely seated in a chair at my usual table.

Another place I would go was Snowdon Delicatessen, I liked it there but would make a lot of noise, and people, of course, would talk about me and stare. "What's wrong with him?" someone would inevitably ask.

Emile once said his aunt or someone saw me in action and reported, "You should have seen the looks he was getting."

Usually people staring stupidly would get me more enraged, and I often avoided busy places when I could. At Murray's I would sit apart from people. And in any case, they would soon move away from me. It was later that I'd learn the technique of delaying tics, yelling, or touching. Touching was especially severe. I would touch, with my hand or my knee, everything. Not breaking but touching—poles, cars, trees, windows, everything around me!

Many times, the violence or a rant-and-rave session had to do with a girl or was the result of anger toward a girlfriend. Most recently, it was Julie who would set me off. One time at her place on Walkley, I got mad at her for some reason and began to kick her cockatiel's cage with the bird in it. Maybe I got mad because her sister was there, and I felt I wasn't getting enough attention. I would get mad at Linda like that a lot if I felt I wasn't getting enough attention. One time, Linda had her friend Denise from Mexico visiting. I came over and got madder and madder.I began to sulk. The real danger was feeling sorry for myself, a feeling that would definitely feed off itself. It would fester and grows till it exploded. By that time, it was too late to avoid a disaster. Girls would have that effect especially.

That was what happened at supper at Lynn's house thirty years ago with her parents and friends. I got mad and started acting belligerent with everybody at the table. Then I made a big display of storming out. That was the last straw with Lynn; things were never the same between us. Things like that with women were almost unavoidable, given my past. I couldn't get close in a healthy way. I think I liked Lynn a lot. She was very pretty and young. But I couldn't have a normal relationship with her. She could, but I couldn't. My attempts at relationships with women would always end in failure.

I don't think I ever liked Linda that much or was ever really infatuated with her. It was after Martha, who saw firsthand all my destructive and violent tendencies. I thought she was very pretty, but many times, I was violent with her. She saw my place or Decarie, so she knew what I was capable of damage-wise. She saw my apartment at its worst. After we broke up, I never saw her again. Nor did I see Katsua.

She used to go to Murray's with me. She would always say, "You can't send me to work without a proper breakfast." I liked going to Murrays with her and liked spending money on her, which she also liked.

She wasn't a good match for me. One time, in my basement apartment, I knocked her unconscious and got really scared. With women, it was almost the same as with damage. It would be like a storm and would blow over, and I would assess the damage I caused.

I gave Martha a lot of things—a TV, carpet, and other things. She would say "I could use that," or, "Give that to me if you're just going to break it." After I would physically abuse her, I would want to make up and would be nice and buy her things.

It was the same when I'd felt self-pity because of lack of attention from Lynn, and I became nasty with her parents. When I got home to Alpine, where I was still living at the time, I called Lynn to make up, but she wouldn't do it again. She gave me the boot.

I had so many girls but never a good relationship. There was Barbar, Ghislair, Corrine, Martha, Katsua, Linda, and finally, followed by Claudia, who turned me onto Dorreen my psychologist. They were all pretty women, different from each other but all nice, and all of them were girlfriend material. But I failed to make relationships with any of them work—with the exception, who I was with the longest. I am still best friends with her, the only time that's ever occurred. All the others would break up with them because I would do things or act in a way that would make them leave.

I've had lots of opportunity to get married. There was Numanzia, a woman from the Dominican Republic who I was seeing behind Martha's back on Decarie. She would have married me. And Barbara wanted to get engaged in the worst way. I'm sure I could have married many of the women I dated, probably because they figured they liked me, and they would be financially secure even if the marriage didn't work out.

And don't forget Audrey when I was living on Alpine. She liked my father and the Jewish newspapers he had. She liked me a lot. And at that time, I wasn't breaking that much. I remember the first time I broke something on Alpine very well. I was trying to punish my father and mother by not going out for supper with them, one of my favorite things. But I started getting madder and madder at them for not taking me with them, even though it was my decision not to go. Finally, not able to stand the anger and self-pity any more, while lying on my bed in my room, I kicked the wall hard and made a hole, which Raymond fixed. That seemed to begin a pattern that, unbeknownst to me at the time would continue for over twenty years—a pattern that would even include Raymond. But I didn't really start breaking a lot till I got kicked out by my mother.

I still remember living with Jerry on my own for the first time and concentrated on my newfound freedom by partying. I thought living apart from my parents I could only do one thing. That is, only one idea came to mind. I would do a lot of drugs. I would play guitar. But mostly, this was a chance to party. I didn't think of being more responsible—didn't consider living on my own with Jerry as a chance to grow up. None of that. I just thought of girls and drugs and music —a lot of grass, hash, and acid.

It was there that it all came unraveled and I had a breakdown. That occurred during a mescaline trip on my own. That's the way I would do most things—alone. I was dating Janet, who thought I was doing much too much acid, she later told my parents. But moving to Overdale was a mistake and mostly Jerry's idea—as was most of my advancement and adventure. Jerry was stronger than me. I can see that in retrospect. And he was better able to go out on his own. Anyway, one day during this period of instability, I asked him to take me to the hospital, but he said he couldn't because he had a class. I don't even think I would have gone but was sort of reaching out. I needed help for sure. And getting it at that time, instead of years later with Dr. Unwin would have been much better. I remember on that mescaline trip for the first time feeling panic and having the thought I might do crazy things such as smash the windows or end up in a hospital.

Nevertheless, I had nobody to turn to. I continued as best I could alone—where I felt most comfortable. Only I couldn't sleep and was afraid and moved back to Alpine. I went running home from my drug-induced breakdown. I felt humiliated and lost. It seemed like the only thing I could do was go home for help. Mostly, it was my identity—as a person who knew all those drugs wouldn't hurt me like everyone said they would—that was wounded. Going home, I felt like they (the straights) had won! I wasn't OK, and I wasn't able to continue. I fell apart. I now wish I had those years to live again. At first, in high school, I'd felt like I was a coward. I'd became afraid of this and had dwelled on this thought constantly. Then I was afraid I couldn't have sex, as that's how I'd felt on Overdale with Janet. And lastly in the trilogy, I'd freaked out, and they had won. By everybody, I meant everybody but my drug-doing friends, like Jerry and Larry. I wasn't right and didn't know as much as I thought I did.

The only person from that era in my life who I've not yet mentioned was the queen of the "on the road songs," Judy Rabinovitch. She was the singer I played with. This was important because it was my chance. This was what I should have been doing. It was my occupation. This was what I should have been concentrating on. We even had some small gigs. I believe the drugs I took were to escape from that duality—go to college for my security and my parents, on the one hand, and what was my strength on the other. I used to go to Bruce's parents' house for a guitar lesson with Bruce and supper. To me, it represented security. I was happy for three hours on Thursdays. So, music was where I was headed and, given that I was good at it and loved it, my obvious choice. I never came to terms with that; I haven't even to this day!

My fear—more than a fear, a panic that terrified me—was that I would go crazy. I avoided everyone I knew who had psychiatric problems, like Eric and David and especially Gary. Even when I thought about them I felt extremely frightened and upset. I would try to avoid them at any cost. It seemed to me maybe I was like them, and that thought was a real downer.

One time on Overdale, some good-looking guy from, I think Ontario, came to our apartment and hit me with two blows. Number one was he was a psychiatric case, a depressive. He told me he would just stay in bed for a month and then said, "There are people who can help you." He remarked on a guy in the hospital he was with who talked to a doctor, and the doctor said, "When you are ready to really talk to me and not take it, come back."

That scared me. It made me think they could force you to get well or make you talk. The other thing that scared me about our exchange was group therapy or, more specifically, wondering, Am I really in that category now? Group therapy, especially at the Jewish General Psychiatric Ward, terrified me. I didn't want to do it. I was afraid they could make you do something you didn't want to do. And above all, I was weaker than everyone else. I liked to hang around normal people like Nathan and Emil. I felt secure at Emil's on Sunday nights jamming with him, which I did for years.

The second thing about this guy from Ontario that was that he played guitar and sang. He said he played with a lead guitarist who was, by the way, much better than me. I didn't show it and hid my feelings, but this statement was so traumatic to me that I still remember it forty years later. The thing was my identity was so shaky and fragile, especially, about being a guitarist, that any comment or situation would and could destroy or shake it. This guy saying that about his friend was a massive blow to my ego. Looking back now, I can see that I had several problems. I was just in the process of becoming an adult, and the drugs I took made the escape from them catastrophic. I was at a crucial stage in my life and was running away from my issues and trying to avoid them. But they caught up with me.

Especially in Holland, where I traveled in 1970, things came to a head. I hadn't smoked dope in a couple of week, and where I was staying, somebody rolled a huge joint out of newspaper. Nobody could smoke it all, but I did. I was also drinking Heineken, and the combination hit me. I started to feel very bad, panicky and out of control. I could or should have talked to someone and looked for a doctor. But I just tried to take it and to deal with it on my own. After that, the rest of my trip was horrible. My identity crisis while I was growing up and my first apartment away from my parents living with Jerry and the drugs were too much for me. I fell apart and even missed an important gig with Marty and Allan.

Traveling to Europe without a plan really and by myself left me unprepared. Also, I broke out in a rash. When I came home, I was a mess after a month. In England, for the second time on the trip, I was broke. I ran out of money and found a bloke to share an apartment or room with. The arrangement was he would buy food and cook for the first week, and I would do the same the next week. But I left without him knowing after the first week. He must have been pissed off. He would come home late at night drunk, and I would be awake but pretended to be asleep.

I was happy when I came home, but I was definitely from an overprotecting family. Every time I would leave home, they would want me to come back. When I used to go to Jerry's on Pinedale and sleep over, my mother would call the police. I definitely was a homebody in a way because my mom and dad both liked to keep me close. Even when I was about fourteen, I used to go with my father to his office and hang around. It must have been about 1966 because I remember going into his tenant's room to play "Rubber Soul" by the Beatles on his record player.

Also, my father used to do abortions, which were illegal then. He would do them in his office on Decarie, and sometimes I would even be in the apartment. One time, I peeked through a crack in the office door and could see a young, pretty woman on the examining table. I don't think at the time I realized what was going on, but I learned as I got older. One time, while he was doing an abortion, something went wrong. The woman started hemorrhaging. The police were called, and they arrested my father. I must have been about fourteen years old. My mother told the reporter there were two young children around, meaning me and my brother, and the reporter promised to keep the incident out of the English papers; they would just put it in the French papers.

My father spent one night in jail, and my mother used that as ammunition when they fought, which was often. I remembered seeing very few displays of affection between them. But when I fought with my mother and swore at her, he would tell me not to, which was the nicest he was to her. I remember violent fights between my mother and everybody else in the house. She harassed my brother so much about his girlfriend he finally moved out. He took a lot of abuse because, as my mother would say, his girlfriend's family wasn't high-class or rich enough (though I believe my mother never set eyes on her). My father was "a stinking European," and it seemed she hated everyone, me included. It was hard to imagine why he'd married her.

For his part, my father ridiculed her and her background. She was from Ottawa and had grown up on a street called York Street. He called her "the Duchess of York," a slur about her lower middle-class upbringing. She had, in fact, had a history of mental instability. Hilda, my aunt, told me, when her mother died before I was born, she'd had a mental breakdown and had been confined to a mental hospital, where she was given shock treatment. My father had bad things about him and would torment my mother, but he'd never had a stay in a mental hospital. Hilda said the only reason my mother was released was because Hilda and Joe had vouched for her.

Things got better for me around 1990—about at the time I met a special woman. Before her, I was embroiled in a physically abusive relationship with Linda. I was also a real estate agent with Royal LePage, Century 21, and Remax, although I sold only one house that whole time. I was also in a band shortly after, and we toured and played around Québec. It was fun and a good experience. In addition, at around that time, I was taking music courses at McGill at night. So, those days with her were sort of a high point in my life.

I went out with Linda for about two years. I'd met her through Robin's connections. I only met her, and she only met me, although we were each supposed to meet three people. Anyway, I was abusive toward her. We went to Nashville and to visit her mother in a trailer home in Alabama. The sex was good, and we would go to our country place. I remember in Alabama getting into a fight with her and her mother. I was sucking like I had with Lynn years before, and her mother told me off, saying that I was a baby. Feeling like this with women was a frequent occurrence when I felt I wasn't getting enough attention. I'm sure it went back to my mother, as she was often in a foul mood.

Anyway, every few days, I would get mad at Linda, probably due to my inability to have a normal relationship. I was always attracted to pretty women. But beyond a certain point, I was incapable of more, and I would become frustrated and angry and eventually hit them. Toward the end of Linda, I enrolled in a group for men with physical abuse problems with women. I remember I did most of the talking in the group. Just like I had been long ago, I was terrified of ending up in the Jewish General. I was also afraid of group therapy. And just like when I had gone to the Allan after a mental breakdown, with Julie calling the police and an ambulance, the reality of it was nowhere near my dread of it. The Allan was actually fun, and so was the group therapy.

When I told the group I'd begun a relationship with a woman who was a kung fu expert, one guy said, "That's your cure right there." And it was. Something about Linda's personality made me want to abuse her. She sort of came across like a victim. But the new womanwas the opposite. She wouldn't stand for my abusive ways, so I had to grow up. And I did. I, myself, broke up with Linda. She didn't want the relationship to end, probably because of her fear of rejection and fear of being dumped. Still, when I took up with her I unequivocally broke up with Linda. But she still loved me, strangely enough, as did Katsua and Martha.

Jumping ahead a bit to when I turned fifty, I had a fiftieth birthday party and invited all my friends. Joey, Emile, Yuri, Julie, and Ron as well as all our musical friends and groupies were there. It was tremendous fun, and I got really drunk. We had the party at G# or Barfly, and I hired the Steve Barry Band to entertain. And later, I jammed with them. The funny thing about the party was it was a great party, but the year that followed was terrible.

My rituals and breaking things were severe that year. I must have broken about five or six windshields in my 1998 BMW. With my next BMW, a 2004, I don't think I broke any. The strange thing was, I would press my knee against the car and make little dents all over it. I devalued the 1998 Bimmer a lot from doing that. I also had a bad accident with it when I was driving to Dorreen's with a coffee. I got distracted with the coffee and smashed into a parked car with two people in it. They thought I'd fallen asleep or something. The police came and drove me to my appointment and talked to Dorreen about me. the people in the car said I'd banged into them twice. The cops did their best to dissuade me from driving, and I had to take a driving test to keep my license.

Julie took me out east very early in the morning, and I drove with an instructor, who would either pass or not pass me. The first thing I did—or, I should say, they first thing they had me do—was put on the parking brake and try to back up. The brake wouldn't stop the car from going like it was supposed to, so I had to go and rent a car. The instructor deemed my car not right and the brake not working properly. I passed the test in the rented car, and it was successful.

Another time more recently, I had to have a medical form filled out to see if I was capable of driving. But I passed that too. And recently, I had to have another form filled out about my medication, which I had done with Dr. Margoliu. So, my driving has been problematic. And it's a problem that goes way back to when I got too many demerit points when I lived on Decarie and lost my license for three months. Another time, an elderly driver saw me swerving and said I had "the ultimate driving machine" with a lousy driver.

Anyway, after my fiftieth party, things for me went downhill. I was seeing Dr. Riven, someone who did me no good, although she probably had good intentions. When I was in the Allan, she called her to inform her of that, and she never called back. Also around that time, I was seeing a black therapist at the Jewish for a while. He would walk with me, but I would still touch everything and bang on windshields of the parked cars.

Another thing I did a lot of was tearing paper. I couldn't read the *Star* or the *Gazette* without tearing the paper repeatedly. And it would be very difficult to read a book without doing the same thing. It was like with breaking glass. I would attempt to see how far I could go without actually ripping the paper. I would always "test it." With paper, I would pull it to get a satisfactory feeling, right up to the point where it would almost rip but not quite. The downside was it would often actually rip. So, I'd end up with a book with half the pages either pulled out or ripped. Newspapers would send me into a frenzy, and I would have newsprint all over my hands. But I would tear money too and valuable papers. Paper money was very dangerous for me. I would often have multiple ripped bills.

I always also had a thing with watches. I loved good watches like Bulova Accutrons and would smash them. I went through a lot of watches that I couldn't leave alone. As with other articles, I would fiddle with them until I was in a rage and then smash them with my hand. The same was true with expensive guitars, the kind I liked. I would buy them, only for them to too often also fall victim to my kicks and knocks. I used to always punch, hammer, and kick my 1940 Martin D-18. And I must have broken 20 telephones, usually into many pieces. I'd return them and say they fell which was a lie.

I had that guitar for many of my destructive years and would get frustrated over not playing well and kick it. One time, I smashed a hole in the side with a kick and had the guitar repaired at Pierre Laporte. There was actually a sizable hole, and the repairman put the pieces back to patch it and did an excellent job. One thing I would do with cars, walls, and glass and not just guitars would be to "knee" something till it gave me satisfaction. I did that with my 1940 D-18 so much there were maybe twenty cracks all over the sides. When I bought the guitar in 1989 it had no cracks in the side, not even one. But I had the urge that was almost a tickle in my knee that would only be satiated by cracking something. I would constantly knee walls and furniture and my guitars, and the D-18 had very thin sides, which is the part I would most like to break. It wasn't as satisfying to knee something that wouldn't break; it had to be fragile like the sides of that guitar. I still do it to this day but not with the same force.

When Julie called the police and ambulance when I had my breakdown eight years ago, I was smashing everything. But the thing that maybe the most satisfying to smash was the Gyprock in the foyer with my knee. I was pretty much out of control and made a hole in the wall. At that point, there was no fooling around or testing. I just smashed the wall with no restraint. Even now, writing about this and thinking about it makes me want to knock something with my knee again. It wasn't an itch exactly but a feeling in my knee that needed to feel something against it with a bit of pressure. The more nervous I am, the more pressure is needed. Right now, I am getting that feeling from thinking about it. So I touch or push the leg of the table with my knee. In the state of mind I'm in now, not much of a push is needed. Also, the longer I delay it, the worse by far it will be. So I do a long succession of bumps to avoid one that could break something. But to me, I absolutely have to feel an object against my knee.I should say here the events this book was written in about 2010, and now it's 2023. Compiled from writings I did over the years but before 2010.

Windows and glass are worse even now. I would say I pretty well know how hard I can hit a window. When I'm out of control, I no longer just want to test but to hit the glass hard enough to break it. Normally, or maybe abnormally, I always think I have to knock windows going up and down the stairs in my house. When I walk up to my bedroom, I feel I have to knock the window at the top of the stairs. It is important to note I see this as a value of a safety feature. The risk is that, if I don't knock all the windows pressure will build up, and I will—or might have to—bang a window with enough pent-up energy or fear as to actually break it. So knocking or kicking something is what prevents me from breaking something. Funny strange how that works.

But I can't forget the rituals. In the front hallway or entrance, there is thin Gyprock I pick on, like the thin sides of an old Martin guitar. I always test it with a small light back kick. But lately, I've been giving it a harder kick. It is interesting to note that, right now, I feel an urge to knock the heel of my right foot on something like the floor or chair, but it doesn't have to be hard. But if I don't do it, say, within a second, the tension will build. There's no way around it. I have these things down to a science and actually know exactly how hard I can hit or kick something.

When I was breaking everything in my bedroom, especially doors or closet doors or my night table, it was at a point where, if I didn't satisfy my urge after only a few seconds had passed, there was an almost certainty I would kick something in a panic with enough force to break whatever object I'd kicked. Delay at this stage would be disastrous. I'm at the stage now where just thinking of the kick or knock will satisfy this urge. In other words, imagining the sensation will be enough. With windows, especially certain ones, the more frantic I get, the harder I hit them. But I can't actually pass certain windows without knocking them twice. The number or repetition is also important. Twice or four times seems to do it, although I used to associate the number four with breaking something. It used to be I had to be at a certain distance from a window, pretty far from it!

Even now, I find myself—besides the windows, which I always knock—kicking things harder. I wonder if writing this (more likely, having it on my mind) is causing this. It worries me a bit, but I hate to stop writing this. Still, it's not out of control to the degree it was thirty, twenty, or even eight years ago. The windshield problem, in particular, was worrisome and very expensive.

The Gyprock and plaster and paint was much less expensive than the labor, which included clean up, throwing Gyprock away, and patching and putting in new sheets. When I had my ground-floor bathroom done, I had the "contractor" put in double sheets of Gyprock. I'd bet, in my life, I've replaced twenty houses of drywall, although this just a guess. At points, repairing and replacing was not just a weekly thing of but, rather, a daily job. But I always felt better and calmer with a repaired wall, rather than one with holes. I actually find broken walls very unsightly and ugly.

I don't know if I already wrote this, but when my father was alive thirty years ago, he said it was costing at least $100 a day to repair and replace what I was breaking. I know it was worrying him greatly, and he hated to think of it. I guess maybe I was a big disappointment to him. But at the same time, he loved me. He was worried, though, and didn't know what to do about it. Many therapists and doctors were found and appointments were set up by him. There was a time, or many times, that he thought I should be in the hospital. I remember one time in particular when he offered to drive me. I lived on Decarie then, both in the basement and in apartment 1.

I would break things in his office. It greatly bothered him when I broke his medical diploma, and I felt bad too. I would have times when I was more relaxed, but lots of times, I resented & hated my father and even made a display of bad behavior and breaking things in front of him. He once said, "Do you like buying a newspaper and then ripping it apart?"

He didn't understand but once said, "You must really hate me."

I feel bad writing and thinking about this. When I remember this, I feel very bad. He thought I was punishing him. And maybe that's was true. I got much worse after he died, though, so maybe then I was mad that he'd died and was gone. The anger and panic got much worse right after he died. Harry tried to step in and help. I told him to go away and offended him by resenting him helping and being at the office. After my father died, no one was left in apartment 6. The Azars moved to another apartment, I think number 4, and I had less to do with them, as they were no longer sharing apartment 6 with my father.

This whole time, a period that lasted from 1979 to 1985, was terrible. I think I was the worst during this period. This was after Ogilvy's and during the time I was seeing my Japanese girlfriend, Katsua. This was the time when I met her, in the Frank Quinn building. It was the time right after my mom kicked me out and the police came and ushered me out of Alpine. My father was in Florida. I was playing in a country band, and it was the era of the Americana towers with Katsua and Cranbrooke and, just after, Decarie. When I was at Frank Quinn's, I was still at Ogilvy's.

At Frank Quinn's, I had that flood when I pulled the sink off the wall or broke the toilet. I don't remember which. It could have been either. I've been known to do both and to break either, especially on Decarie in the basement apartment. At that time, just like I had Raymond for walls and furniture, I had Bill the plumber for plumbing problems. He was shocked by what I broke. But like Raymond, he made a lot of money with me. He also came nights and weekends, almost a friend. He eventually bought the building at 4620 Decarie after my father died and wanted to buy our house at Alpine too.

Writing like this that I'm doing now would have been either very problematic or impossible back in those days. I remember trying to enter the books in my father's office and repeatedly crossing things out and tearing the pages. My father had me do a few simple things, like going through the building and collecting rents. Also I went around to the other buildings my father owned. I collected rents, saw if something needed fixing, and called the repair person. Some of the slums on St. Catherine East were in terrible shape and needed lots of work.

When my father was around, we'd often drive out to St. Catherine East together. He was trying to get me "a feel" for real estate. One time at the building near Moreau, there was a tenant who was ruining the place and not paying rent. He was in jail for a while, as was the guy in charge of the roaming house on St. Cathedral Street near St. Laurent. There were definitely tough and unsavory people at these buildings.

There was also a Portuguese restaurant on the corner of St. Cath and St. Laurent. It was a nice place with pretty girls, who were the owner's daughters. I would go there and drink at the bar and flirt with the girls, one of whom got sick and died at a very young age. They were both very pretty. They didn't like that I was there collecting the rent and mostly complained about things being broken in the building and things like leaks, which happened often.

On Moreau, the guy who was in jail threatened me after I snuck into his apartment by the back, saying he'd kill me if I came back. He said, "If you come back into my apartment upstairs again, you won't be able to walk down the stairs." I knew he meant he'd kill me. The other guy who was in jail at St. Laurent was operating a roaming house with rooms mostly being used for prostitutes. These were the type of places my father sent me too and he owned. I didn't break things there, though. I waited till I was home. But I got used to being a slum lord! It was hard work.

I used to break, tear, and bend things. It would feed off itself. One time when I was seeing Martha, and in fact on the way to her place, a hooker was hitchhiking and I picked her up. At this point in my life, twenty-five years ago, I had never paid for sex. Of course, we always pay indirectly for sex with a wife or girlfriend, but I had never paid a hooker. If the opportunity presented itself now, I would jump at the chance. But at that time, I thought something bad would happen to me if I went to a prostitute. Or more likely, I would have to break something as a result. This type of chain reaction, in fact, was very prevalent and happened constantly. If I did a certain thing, there would be serious repercussions—everywhere and all the time. If I did a certain thing in my car—let's say I didn't swerve for example, I would have to hit the windshield. Rituals.

Another thing I found it hard to do was hygiene—taking a bath, shaving, and brushing my teeth. They were all riddled with rituals. so I avoided them and stayed dirty. Lori said to take a shower every two days, which I do now. But at that time, it was very hard. I had rituals with the soap, the bathroom, and the washing itself. I would only brush my teeth occasionally, and when I went to a dentist in the late '70s, I had tons of cavities. Even going to the bathroom or into the bathroom was hard. I preferred sinks that had supports or legs because, if they were just attached to the wall, I would put pressure on them and "test" them to see how far I could go. I would push the sink down. And the vanity mirror was a huge problem. I don't know how many I broke in different apartments and had to replace. I would hit them,and the thinners ones would break easily. It was my thing with glass, and it extended to the glass in picture frames and fixtures for lighting. Even on Alpine, I was drawn to those long light fixtures with the thin sides that were easy to bend, so even on Alpine I was doing those kinds of things.

Later on, it got worse. I would break many glass objects. Glass, to me, was always a temptation. But I rarely felt good or happy. It was ritual and anger that made me push, bend, or squeeze things. And somehow, I always felt bad and was shocked when whatever I was testing would break. Anybody else would say, "It's glass. Of course it will break." But I developed a feeling for how much I could push or how hard a knock would actually shatter various types of glass and glass objects. Sinks too. I would push down on them, testing them and pushing harder by increments. They would at last break, but when that happened, it would scare me.

But still I loved getting up and walking to Murray's. At the time, I did no actual exercise and, therefore, had tons of energy, anger, and frustration. Mandy once said to me, on the phone, "If I didn't do any exercise, I would be the same as you are." One doctor, Dr. Pernicki (actually, Mila Muroney's father) told me, "Go to the Y and workout." I thought at the time, *What a stupid thing to say. I can't go there with so many rituals.* But he was right. It would have been hard but beneficial. Years later, in the 1990s, I joined Nautilus and felt much better. But there were lots of rituals and yelling. People would look at me. But eventually, they would get used to me, and the whole thing was *very* helpful. Even now that I no longer belong to the Y, I do exercises. But on Decarie I walked.

The walk was very full of stops to touch stones and things on the street, though. I could barely go for ten seconds uninterrupted. I would count everything and was almost oblivious to reality or my surroundings. One time on Decarie, a neighbor said about me, "He doesn't know what he's doing," which was, in some way, true.

One of the hardest and worst feeling things I did on Decarie was the garbage and the laundry. It was tortuous. The task of taking clothes from the machine and to the machine was laden with doing and undoing. It was terrible. I would touch the walls and smash the washer and dryer out of frustration and carry the washed clothes to apartment 1 sometime ten times. Usually the frustration became too much for me, and I would kick and smash everything along the way. If I could do anything only once or twice, it was considered a huge victory.

Also, as I did these rituals in public, people would inevitably watch me or stare at me—most people but not everyone. I did encounter some people who understood a bit or were sensitive to my dilemma, but they were rare. One was the beautiful black woman who I later identified as a hooker or, more accurately, a call girl. She was very nice to me. I think if I had availed myself of her services, I would have felt better, and it would have benefited me.

Near Murray's, there was a group of stores—the gift shop, Magic Touch stereo, the magazine shop, Joe's lunch Counter, and the Bank of Montreal. I frequented all of these businesses on a regular basis, and I was at the bank daily. I loved to look at and buy the products at Magic Touch. When I bought my first really good car, a Datsun 240 SX, it had no stereo, and I loved nothing better than to go to Magic Touch and look for a radio to put in the car in the passenger seat. Funny strange that, with all the damage I later did to that car, I didn't want to hurt it by installing a stereo. It was also strange—or maybe not—that I loved having good, unbroken things. I broke so much after all. That was why I kept replacing and fixing things. Whenever I broke a TV or boom box or clock, it was a tribute to my resilience that I would come back to life and buy a new one. It was like a fresh start. This is what my life was. I would become enraged and go into a fury. Then I'd settle down and take stock of what I'd broken. This continued right to Beaconsfield up to six years ago.

One technique I developed over the years was to kick or knock something that wasn't breakable or dangerous, like a table or the floor. And another technique was thinking about or imagining breaking something. Instead of knocking or punching a window, I would imagine doing so. This would often satisfy my urge, and as time went by, this technique became second nature.

I liked to sit on the little metal fence, just like the "crazy" guy from upstairs would do. He had some kind of physically crippling problem, but he would sit outside on the post. Later on, I would do it, too, and it relaxed me a bit. Often, if I was stationary and not near anything breakable, I could relax. But as soon as I was moving, there were a thousand obstacles for me to pass. If I walked down the front walkway, there would be lots of rituals, and I would touch everything, if not knock things. Usually, the difference between touching and hitting was a degree of anger and loss of patience. There are only so many things you can touch and so many rituals you can do before you will lash out at something. It got frustrating and, around people, worse.

When I was alone, though, it was worse in another way, as I could break and "test" things to my heart's content. There was no one to watch or prevent me from this violent, destructive behavior.

Definitely, being alone in my apartment was worse, except when I lived with Katsua. One time, we had a glass table—a glass top. I would push down on it. One time, I pushed too hard on it with Katsua there, and it smashed. Also, I remember one time with Katsua, I threw an Arcoroc—a thick tumbler—against the wall. And as those type of glasses would tend to do, it shattered into a million pieces. Another time, I was making a lot of noise kicking things in the American Towers with Katsua, and the man from downstairs accosted Katsua in front of me, saying, "What are you doing to him?" This was very humiliating for me and a threatening and violent experience for Katsua. She started to cry when he was yelling at her. When I remember this incident, I'm ashamed of myself for not sticking up for her and protecting her.

Another thing I did a lot of was honk in my little Datsun B-210. One time, we drove it to Washington, DC. We were in a tough neighborhood, and there was a tough-looking black guy, and I honked at him. If he would have gotten a hold of me, it would have been the end. One time with Martha, I was driving along the boulevard, and I swerved and honked at a guy on a skateboard. I scared the shit out of him. He jumped off his skateboard onto the sidewalk. Back then, fifteen or twenty-five years ago, I would always get into fights in my car. Looking back, I realize I had a lot of close calls.

One thing that was hard or impossible to do was hold things in after a certain point of anger. If I got worked up, and I was holding back a yell or a knock, it would have to come out. The longer the delay, the worse the results. It would be ugly. If something didn't go my way and a reaction didn't happen, it was bad news, especially if I was already nervous or in a state. If I felt stronger, there would be less to "make up."

That was why, when I had my breakdown, the reaction time was extremely short. I was out of control. It was a horrendous day. I was smashing everything with no reaction time or delay. There was no relief. Julie called the police and asked for an ambulance to be sent. The ambulance guys were afraid to come in without the police, but in fact, I was more dangerous to myself than I was to anyone else. I was a danger to the house and its contents, not really to people like Julie or the ambulance guys.

It was always my biggest fear that I would end up in a psychiatric ward or hospital, so I was petrified and shocked when I heard Julie say she was calling 9-1-1 for an ambulance. I couldn't get past my fear that, after thirty years, I was really going to be in a mental hospital. It was an obsession and dread at work here. When I heard Julie call for them I was panic-stricken. Finally, I was really going to stay in a hospital. It was donning on me that I was virtually in a hospital, and when the ambulance was making its way along Cote St. Luc Road with me inside, I felt scared, really scared, like it was finally happening. But the whole thing was strange because it wasn't as bad as I had always feared; the reality and facing it was not nearly as bad as the fear and dread I had cultivated over thirty years. First,we went to the Jewish General, where the staff could process me, and I was put in emergency, where they could decide what to do with me.

As relieving and as nice it was to go to Murray's, it was equally great when my girlfriend took off work and came to see me in the emergency of the Jewish General Hospital. I'll never forget how good it was to see her. I wasn't alone. But I cried, "I don't want to be here." Still, it was relief and happiness that I felt after a long time with her visits.

Next, I was sent to the Allan, another place of my nightmares. But none of all this compared to the fear I had built up since I was twenty. At the Allan, I was put in a room with two other guys who seemed twenty times as bad as me. I was a bit afraid of sharing a room, but I soon got my own room across the hall. Most of the people staying at the Allan were long-termers and heavily sedated, but I was almost having fun there. The terror of being confined to the Allan disappeared when I faced the reality of the situation. I was having fun!

When I was at the Allan, all the doctors and interns wanted to interview me because I was so articulate. They wanted to talk to me to get an idea of mental illness, and I was happy to converse with them. It was a very good thing to confront my dread head-on. When I was in a bad way on Overdale and, later, home on Alpine, I worried and obsessed over being in a psychiatric ward. But I only wish now I'd have gone back then and dispersed my tears. I was living in fear of people, sex, and acid. And I could have faced it after all. The fear and dread were much, much worse than the reality. Maybe back then it would have been awful to be in a hospital. But if my stay in the Allan was any kind of example, it would definitely be an anticlimax. In the Allan, there would be activities and exercises, but nobody made me do anything.

The best thing that came out of the Allan was a review of my medication. They even attended to my psoriasis and a cut on my hand that I'd gotten during my breakdown. Could have been from anything, that cut, but it wasn't a bad one.

The meals were good, and I had fun. I was dressed normally, and I would go down to the coffee shop, which I liked. I'd always liked restaurants and coffee shops ever since I was a kid. We used to eat out twice a week on Alpine. My mother wouldn't cook, often saying, "You are on your own tonight. I'm going to a movie." And I was always happy to eat out with my father. At first, Donald would come with us. But after a while, he drifted apart and did his own thing, like studying in the library. We would go to Piazza Tomasso, the Fireside, and the Brown Derby. I loved going out with my father and looked forward to it. No doubt those times were the basis for me ordering supper all the time now. It seemed special. I still love ordering, but I don't go to restaurants very much anymore because, with my yelling, it's hard.

When Donald drifted away from the family and was hardly ever home, I always thought I would get more attention and freedom in the house. But it wasn't what I thought. I felt lonely and, for some reason, lost direction. I could go in his room and have the house and my father to myself; but it didn't exactly work out that way. I kind of missed him. He was very nice to me when I was freaking out, and he would talk to me.

Even then bicycles and riding were a big part of his life, and he was less babied and tougher than me. He would ride to McGill on his bike at seven in the morning in the rain. He had a mental toughness and was not kept so close to my parents. Every summer, you'd see him with his backpack hitchhiking out west of Canada at the corner of Decarie and Cote St. Luc Road. I would hang around my father, mother, and friends instead.

When I lived on Alpine, I used to bicycle myself, and I liked it before I drove. Now, I have a car, a scooter, and a bicycle, and I use them all. When I was a kid, I dreamed of a Torpado 5 or a 10-speed racer. They were the coolest things. I guess I was about fourteen or fifteen when I lusted after a bike like that. Donald got a twenty-speed bike, and I got a cheap but good Czech bike that I loved. When I graduated from Sir George, I got a Peugeot ten-speed bike with a light and fenders. That was kind of like my present for graduating. I was now mobile, and I rode it a lot.

Not long after that, I got a driver's license and would drive the Nova, which I also loved. The Nova seemed as cool as the bike, but it was my mother's. Before the 1976 Nova, we had a Rambler American convertible, which was also neat. I think, in 1966, my father bought a new gold '66 Toronado, the first year they came out. There was nothing I loved better than to go car shopping with Dad, and I used to love going to showrooms.

Actually, I liked to hang around my father anytime—going for supper, going to the office, and just talking. I was attached to him and to my mother, but in different ways. My father could look after me in a moral and financial way. He would give me $20 a week allowance. Later, when I got older, he upped that to $100 and then $200. I didn't really need the money they paid me at Ogilvy's, and my dad always wanted me to quit and work with him. But there was never that much to do at the office, although I did have some duties. Those ranged from filling out and entering details into the books, going around and collecting rents, and going down to Queen Mary to do the banking. After I got fired from Ogilvy's, I got even more attached to my dad, and my official capacity was working with my father. I would also go to the country with him, which I liked. In general, I felt secure around him. He could supply me with money, and I felt definitely "protected" around him.

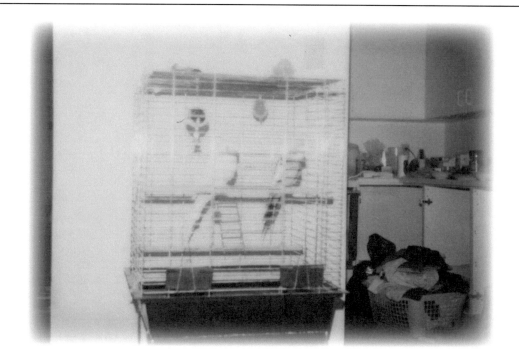

Really, music and playing guitar were what I was best at and should have been doing. But Dad discouraged me from pursuing that interest. I had many opportunities then and later to play with people. I used to jam and play with Ronnie and Allan who made it clear I was second choice behind Bobby. One time, there was a gig on Sir Winston and they asked me to audition for the gig, but Allan made his preference very clear.

I resented my father for keeping me close to him and, at the same time, tried to get around seeing music as a profession and followed his wishes for me. I hung around the office and "got a feel for real estate." Anyway, my father always wanted me to go into commerce. But I hated him and resented him for keeping me so close to him and for keeping me from finding my own way and moving out and making my way in the world. Music was definitely what I was cut out for. From an early age, I was dealing in guitars.

It was clear there were distinct roles and expectations for me and Donald, and they were vastly different. Donald was wanted but not really overprotected. He was the older one and could go his own way, although he was persecuted by my mother but treated well by my father. My father would brag about him. "He's a six-footer, and he's going to be a doctor." My father didn't ever say, "Brian's a great guitarist, and he's going to be a musician."

My mother was more likely to be sympathetic toward my musical proclivities. She used to like to hear me play and listen to me. In my parents' bedroom, she would be on her bed, and I would sit on my father's bed and serenade her. In a way, she was the softer of the two, although she was a terror. She could be kind.

Although it seemed like my father was persecuted by my mother, he was often not nice to her. He actually persecuted her and would insult her terribly. He would criticize her poor background and call her crazy. At the time, it seemed like my mother was the "bad" one. But now I can see, looking back, that my father was mean to her. It was easy at the time to blame my mother because she had mental and skin issues and was often out of control. She had a very bad case of psoriasis that tortured her mentally, and she was very nervous and fearful, which negatively colored her disposition. My father would call her cockeyed but come to her defense when I got overly offensive in a fight with her. He would say, "Don't be so rough," and, "Don't use such rough language with her." He would come to her defense. But, to me, it was a mismatch and mystery why he married her. I was a companion to both of them. I would hang around my father for security and was close emotionally to my mother.

Donald was going to be the successful one. I, because it worked that way, was going to be the problem and the failure. It is little surprise to me I acted out and lived my role—the negative one—balancing out the family. Although my father was very proud of Donald, they weren't really close. And Donald never seemed to be close to my mother like I was. I depended much more on my parents than Donald did. He got his own car first, a green 1977 Honda Civic, one of the first years for them. I got my own car, too, and at a really good deal, a 1976 Datsun B-210. That mine was the good deal wasn't surprising. I was the more money conscious, although I was only a musician. I got this car and a stereo, a TV, skis, and other things all for $2,000 from a friend of Katsua's who needed the $2,000 to get back to Japan. It was a great deal, and the car only a few thousand miles on it. It was in perfect condition, and the deal was in keeping with the idea and fact that I had a talent for deals or buying and selling.

Funny thing, even though Donald was going to be a doctor and have great earning power, I might have been the more money minded. I was better with wheeling and dealing, though Donald had more money than I did because of his profession. Still, I was talented and very much had a mind for money. I was more than a bit like my father in that way. My hankering for collectables and my guitar playing came from him, too. I'm sure I have money matters in my blood.

My father was deeply worried about my behavior and my breaking things. At times, I think it made him sick and killed him. But that's bullshit. He was tough but was eighty-seven and had diabetes. So, I didn't kill him with worry as I sometimes feared. Still, I knew he was very worried and not about me drinking. He thought that maybe I was taking drugs. But what really bothered him, I think, was me breaking everything.

I think, in a fragile way, he loved me even more than Donald. But maybe that's not the case. Nevertheless, I was very close to him. I spent much more time watching TV with him than Donald did. I would walk to Queen Mary with him to the bank, and sometimes we'd eat together at Woolworth's Counter. And every Saturday, we had lunch at Pumpernick's when it was on Decarie.

I don't think I was as bad as he imagined, but I wasn't nice to him. When he felt sick a few months before he died, he wanted me to drive him to the hospital, but I wouldn't. I told him to take a taxi. I think he did. I could have driven him. After all, he was my father. But I didn't, and I feel bad about it now. I had issues with my driving. My mother was with him every day in the hospital and was a dutiful wife. Even Uncle Joe came to see him, and he was almost crippled with his hip and had a very time walking and getting around. He came from Ottawa by bus.

When my mother died, it was over twenty years later, and we didn't have a Shiva. We didn't go to great lengths for our parents it seems. When my mother died five years ago, it was far different for me than when my father died. It was a different era; twenty years had passed.

My father died at a very bad time for me. I was still breaking everything. I may not have even been taking Anafranil yet, which was a turning point for me. I was probably seeing Dr. Pecknold at St. Mary's, and it was definitely before I started seeing Lori I was getting into fights and was living on Decarie. It was one of my worst periods.

When my mother died, I was firmly and safely ensconced in my house on Beaconsfield. The only trouble I had with people on Beaconsfield was with my next-door neighbors, who were Indian. The father attacked me and called me a lousy neighbor. When I said, "Fuck off," he jumped on me. Our feud even ended up in court after I called the police. I am convinced he picked on me and had no respect for me because he saw I was alone and had mental issues. He even asked me once if Linda was my social worker. What an asshole. I had lots of trouble with his whole family, and that remained so till he moved away ten years ago. Actually, to tell the truth he had a reason to consider me a bad neighbor. I did nothing about the dead tree whose branch broke off and fell on his roof. If something like that happened now, I would definitely call a tree guy.

My other neighbors on the other side were always nice. When I first moved in, I met Sarah and Tony and their two kids right away. One was Rachel. I remembered her name because she had dark hair like Rachel Welch. They were excellent neighbors and were nice to me and never bothered me. After them came Bob, who later died of cancer sadly, Bob. He was a great neighbor too. Now, there is another young family with two young children, like Tony and Sarah, and they, too, are no problem. And I could have trouble with neighbors, because I honk a lot and yell and make noise and have tics. Where the Indians lived is now occupied by Billy and his wife and young kids. I have the most contact with them of all my neighbors. Billy helps me fix and assemble things, and this winter, he will do my snow. In summer, he mows my front yard, and I do the back. The only problem with him is everything is his business. When I'm having some work, he has to know how much it cost. He's very nosy but helpful. Still, I tell him everything he asks me and bend over backward not to have a bad relationship with him. He's OK and changed my scooter battery for me. The black woman across the street used to be very nosy. She was the one in the neighborhood who knew everything about everybody. I don't know if she's still like that, as she's getting much older, and her husband died. But she used to be among the nosiest of people out there.

My other neighbor, Mary, who lives two houses away, is hot even though she's sixty-three or sixty-four. Really, I guess, I have the most to do with her socially. We go to the Wheel Club together, and she comes over to my house. But unlike Billy, she's not nosy. Still I keep an arm's length from her and avoid shtupping her. If she lived somewhere else, I would try to schtupp her. But seeing how she's so close to me, I avoid it. But her and her friend Martha, who I've asked out, came over to my house a while back, and we all got drunk on scotch. They started moving my furniture around. Mary and Martha got really drunk, and so did I but not as slashed as them. They are both nice, but we keep a distance.

So, that's a big reason I live here—the neighbors accept me, and there's no trouble like there used to be on Decarie and Richmond. When I so much as think about Richmond, I shudder. That might have been one of the worst places for me. Maybe it's tied for worse with Cranbrooke. But both Cranbrooke and Richmond were years ago. Back then I was much worse, but in both those places, I was very close and attached to neighbors. My house now is completely separate. When I bought Richmond, I was on Decarie, and the brand-new building tempted me, its newness appealing to me. I didn't realistically consider the obvious problem of having neighbors in the same building. I should have bought a detached house like I did after that. Elaine was the real estate agent who found me my house. I think she was scared of me. She just wanted to make a sale. But it was the best thing I ever did. And I have been here now for exactly twenty-five years.

I love my surroundings and am in a very good situation. I have privacy, which is essential for me, and feel comfortable where I am and, more importantly, secure. The need for security and a feeling of safety led me to certain security improvements I made when I first moved here. The first thing I did to feel safe was install bars on the basement windows, gratings on the glass on the front and side doors, and a metal iron gate on my patio door. I had been robbed repeatedly on Decarie and each time felt like a very deep violation of myself. I wanted to do everything I could to avoid being robbed again and wanted to feel safe. These improvements helped somewhat, but my place on Beaconsfield was broken into twice anyway. Both times, much less was taken than had been on Decarie, but I was sad and pissed off anyway. I also got an AD7 alarm system, which increased my feeling of well-being. A feeling of well-being was what I'd been looking for ever since I left Alpine—and it had proven very illusive. I suppose I would most like to live in a castle where anybody else is barred from coming. When the Indian neighbors were here one time, the father tried to get at me through the patio door. I felt very vulnerable. His action was a violation of my privacy. Ideally, I would like to have a house with doors and windows that would all be barred. But there is always a way in.

More about eight years ago when I had that series of incidents at the Jewish General Hospital. I was seeing a black man as a therapist. After seeing him in his office, I went to the hospital for prescriptions or something like that. I had to wait a long time, and the longer I waited, the more agitated I became. Finally, I saw Dr. Brown, who I used to see at his office. Not understanding me, he suggested I go outside for a walk or something. It was during this outing that I became enraged and was yelling and hitting or kicking everything I came across. People were looking at me like I was crazy, and I became less and less in control. As I was walking along the driveway to emergency, I hit an ambulance window and cracked the glass with my hand. Luckily no one saw me do this. I tried as best I could to get to the street and get a taxi. By this time, I was in a full-blown rage and got a taxi and broke the door handle from the inside of the cab. At last, I got home, where I wreaked more havoc in my room, breaking and kicking several things. I finally calmed down, probably taking a pill. And I think I managed to fall asleep and felt much better when I awoke.

I saw Steven and Anne today for lunch. We had a good time, but I got diarrhea when I got home. I wanted to walk home, but I had to go to the bathroom and couldn't wait, so I took a taxi. We talked about everything in my life. And I even got the erroneous impression they might have been jealous, as I was doing so many things and was doing well. I told them about my art, my gig at Knolten, my finances, and my home improvements. It is possible (and maybe even likely) that someone may be jealous to hear all that. But in Steven and Anne's case I don't believe so. They are good people and were a bit surprised I don't see more of my family, which is weird I guess, especially since Paul lives close and David wants to be a guitarist. I will have to rectify that and spend some time with Paul, Clare, and David.

I don't know why I've never seen much of my nephews and niece and now see Donald, Monique, and the kids even less. When we still had the cottage, I would go up there with different people, like Julie or Diane, and visit Sherbrooke as long as I was up there. But I could take Diane to Ottawa or Sherbrooke, and we'd see them.

I miss the cottage and have a lot of memories there, mostly good ones of my parents, especially my father. I used to love to swim, go shopping in Magog, and go boating. Maybe it's good we sold the cottage, but we did so when the real estate market was bad and there were so many other cottages for sale as well. It would have been the time to buy and not sell. I guess, in our family, we choose to avoid each other and not think about our family—and especially about the past. But right now, the past seems good. That's not to say the present isn't better than ever.

When we sold the cottage nine or ten years ago, I was in a bad way. I remember the day of the signing. I had a very hard time driving to Sherbrooke. That time was a low point in the last twelve years, and I wouldn't have driven up if Donald hadn't insisted. He said, "You have to come up. If you can't drive, take a bus." He was tough with me. Anyway, I went by car but now regret selling the cottage. I should definitely have bought Donald's half off of him if he didn't want it. When I drove up to empty the cottage or take a few things, like the Monopoly game and lamp, I pressed against the glass over the bedroom picture and smashed it. At that time, I was breaking a lot of things—like walls and the windshields of my 1998 BMW, the first BMW I had. It was a bad time, like I said. I think I was still sort of but not really and was in between girls. It was before Julie or Diane, as she might have been in Toronto. I think it was just about the time I met Julie. And my house on Beaconsfield was kind of a mess but not as bad as twenty-five years ago then. I also avoided going to see Steven in Ottawa. He is one member of the family who frequently makes overtures about getting together!

It seemed like only shortly before my mother died that I went to the Allan. But I kind of see these two events as having happened simultaneously. It was a very good thing, the Allan, for two reasons. One was the opportunity to confront my fears of psychiatric hospitals. And the second was a revision of my pills or medication. Before the Allan, I was seen by Dr. Riven, and she put me on Ritalin. At the same time, I was seeing Claudia. Back then, I had my Gilchrist mandolin, which I loved and treasured—though, at the same time, I was very rough with it. Anyway, I kicked the case with the mandolin in it very hard, probably partly due to the Ritalin and partially because of fear and anxiety. Anyway, I badly cracked and damaged the top of the Gilchrist and felt terrible. So, I took two courses of action. One, I stopped the Ritalin. And two, I broke up with Claudia, who didn't see why we should break up. She said sandal season was over. With me not saying cunt anymore or staring at women's feet, as the summer was over, we would be OK. But in my mind, I connected the three—breaking the mandolin, Dr. Riven and the Ritalin, and my anxiety over my relationship with Claudia. Claudia had agreed with Dr. Riven and thought I should give the Ritalin a chance. Anyway, one good thing did come out of seeing Claudia, who I liked. Through her, I found Dorreen who I soon started to see as my therapist.

In actuality, although these events are run together in my mind, they didn't all happen at the same time. I wish I knew the time frame better. I do know that Claudia, Dr. Riven, and the Gilchrist mandolin which I sold to Mike must have happened before my mother died. Mom died in 2005. And I know they happened slightly before the Allan, as Claudia was long gone by then. Claudia and Dr. Riven must have happened around 2000. The Allan must have been 2002 or so. Anyway, Claudia was the first girl I went out with and slept with after another big event, not going out with girls anymore. I was always looking for someone else as a distraction when I was seeing her. And I found Claudia on Lavalife. But I liked Claudia. And if not for my "cunts," things would have been better between us.

To reiterate, in more recent memory, I hold the craziest and most dangerous girl I've ever known. And I've been with some crazy ones. Take Ilana. She threw me out of her apartment naked and spilled a liter of bottled water over me in bed. And she had multiple orgasms from being touched. But Marcella was much, much worse and infinitely more dangerous. I met Marcella at around closing time at Spurs when I was in a country band playing there. She looked good, so I hit on her. But she wasn't interested in me. She was into Joey, the lead singer. (What else is new?) Anyway, I gave her a ride home—which I shouldn't have done, as I was pretty loaded—and I remembered where she lived. I thought about her in the next month, often. One time, I was near MTH west, and I got up the courage to leave a note in her mailbox. But she was home, so she opened the door and talked to me. She then gave me her number. I must say I'm attracted to girls who are unstable and dangerous, exactly like her. We went out to Spurs again, and it was on this night that she got really drunk and physically assaulted the barman and the doorman. I was literally restraining her from hitting anyone else, and she got kicked out of the club and was banned from even coming back.

The story of Marcella gets weirder. About six months later—I believe it was the summer of 2009—I bought a 1939 Martin D-28 guitar, which was worth upwards of $75,000, and had it shipped to a friend in Malone, in New York. Because I don't like driving, I asked Marcella if she would drive and go with me to bring it back over the border. I knew something was up when she arrived forty minutes late and had obviously been drinking. I should have known when, at the border entering the United States, she lied immediately and said we were visiting a friend of hers that things were not going to go well. The truth was we were going to Malone to pick up my guitar. Why not just say that? Her lie was a harbinger of things to come. Anyway, finally and luckily we got through the border and made our way to Malone, where Dave welcomed us and offered us tequila, which Marcella didn't refuse.

With my drug- and life-induced breakdown, I felt less of myself. I was down on myself for not being in control. Before this, I had obsessions that would last for years. This time, my obsession was that I was weak and less than perfect and strong like I'd previously thought. The only thing that alleviated the pain was Valium, although I was put on Elavil and Ativan and twenty other antipsychotics, tranquilizers, and antidepressants. Like I said, Valium would help, but only when I took it now and then. I wouldn't discover the pill that would help the most until years later—Anafranil, prescribed by Dr. Pecknold, also with a first name John, like Unwin. But this was when I was thirty.

Unwin thought I should leave home and maybe share a place, but I never did. I did "run away from home" to Atlantic City in 1974 at age twenty-two for a month or more. When I imagined a vacation, this was what came to mind. It was a trip I could relate to, as I had gone there with my family years earlier. I took a bus and stayed for about six weeks at a motel, where I was raped by a woman and met a fellow musician, John Fields. We played together, and he thought my lead playing was the perfect foil for his songwriting, singing, and guitar playing.

Years later, probably at age thirty, I saw another doctor my father found. Heine was the doctor who introduced psychotropic medicine to North America. I remember well that he said, "You're not a stupid person. You know you will be taking medication for the rest of your life." And he was right!

Another thing that happened was I preferred to spend my time with old people, not people my age like I used to. I liked to hang around my father's office and see older visitors, like Lou and my father and Bruno. This was part of my forsaking the life and people who had previously been part of my life. I also liked to watch old movies and spend time by myself. My life was very much a succession of ups and downs, but whichever stage I was in, it was extreme. After feeling extreme mental anguish, I would end up after enough of that in a euphoric period of trying to go back in time and recapture those times when I was independent. This included the country, old friends, and Ron's house in Hampstead, anything to distract me from my thoughts. I particularly liked going out for supper. Even now, my dreams are full of scenes. In them, I find my father; my mother (sexual); and Jerry and Ron, my two oldest and closest friends. What I didn't realize was what happened to me was not something wrong but, rather, a long interruption of my real life.

In most of my dreams in the present time, my mother takes on the role of an out-of-control, angry crazy person. She is usually true to life and irate and furious and out of control. She usually has a vendetta against and hates, or seems to hate, everybody. Sometimes, she is almost normal, when she's caught off guard—at which time, I believe, she is really herself. She is cashing in money at the bank sometimes. My father is smart but very fragile. He's an old man who has a hard time driving because of his age and limited faculties. Often, he explains things to me and is very clever and knowledgeable.

Most of my dreams take place on Alpine or Decarie but often Alpine. Last night,in my dream, there was a "normal" scene on Alpine in the basement, where I would play guitar and where my amps were. A guy who was a seller sometimes and a musician came over for a band practice, and there was a beautiful girl whose name I forgot, so I couldn't introduce them. This forgetting of names is prevalent in my dreams, as well as in real life. Anyway, she must have been living with us on Alpine because she was at home there. I remembered the musician's name but not hers. The guy, who I'd bought musical stuff from before, was selling an early '50's tele with case, and I remarked that the case alone must be worth $2,500. He countered, "More than that." So, I had an idea he knew well what his stuff must be worth. But he was a nice guy, and I liked him.

My father taught me something also last night. Lifelike, he told me the prime interest rate was going up a quarter of a percent. I responded by saying, "That's nothing because the mortgage rate will only rise by the same increase, a quarter of a percent, which was a joke and negligible." But he countered that it didn't work that way. The increase could be 2 percent or 4.5 percent from the mortgage rate up to as much as 6.5 percent. That's the way it worked. I'm not convinced. In real life, he might be wrong. It might be based in reality.

Anyway, we had a practice. And I was happy and proud about the pretty girl staying with me. Also, I saw my mother outside at this time. I ran into her while putting something outside. She was uncharacteristically nice, which I think was because I'd caught her outside. In real life, she would have been fuming about the girl in the basement, as she had done in real life with two girls in the past, Barbara and another girl from Boston who I'd met through a friend at Sir George University. Both were made most unwelcome by my mother, especially the friend's friend. My mother was in a rage—why, I don't know—and she threw her out. She said, "Your train is coming. And don't think you can stay here another day." I was extremely embarrassed and can only imagine what the girl thought about me and my mother. I'd invited her into my home, and she was treated this way. Barbara, too, was unceremoniously thrown out and wasn't allowed to use the washing machine, as she might break it. I think now as I'm writing this my mother saw these two girls as competition and hated them and treated them as such—as rivals who would come between her and her son. This is not so unusual, except for the anger and resentment and the fact that, years later, she would throw out of her house and life the son she had seen as her mate—the very person whose attention the girls, in her mind, were rivals for.

Going hand in hand with keeping me tied to my mother's apron strings was keeping me away from others she deemed unacceptable. She always liked Ronnie Hier because his mother was of a higher social status than herself. But his family wasn't really richer than us. They just lived better and lived in a nicer house and spent more money. One time, Philip's mother called mine after he told his mother I took drugs. His mother called mine about that. Gerry was never considered as socially high as the Hiers were. She didn't particularly like Jerry, and there were issues when I would sleep over at his house. But if I slept at Ronnie's house, there would be no problem.

One time Ronnie, his sister, Ronnie and I went to Atlantic City. It was fun. Ronnie was Joanne's boyfriend, but people made it known that it could have been me in Abrams's situation, mostly because I had gone out with Joanne once. Since then, Mrs. Hier said I had my chance. I used to love going over to their house in Hampstead. Hier was my best friend and also my musical partner. He was multitalented—splitting his efforts between drawing cartoons, photography, and music. He played a bit of piano and was very adept at guitar and most adept at drums. We used to switch instruments in his basement on Glenmore and spent a lot of time together listening to music, talking, and going out. During this period, I hadn't yet got my driver's license. So, Ronnie drove and always said I owed him ten years of lifts. But by the time I got my license, we were no longer so close, as he'd moved away—first to Los Angeles and later to Toronto. But I would see him summers.

I always felt good and secure when I would go to his house in Hampstead and loved the things we would occupy ourselves with, playing Monopoly, talking about and listening to music, and stuff like that. When he visited me on Richmond in the '80s, I played pedal steel for him, and we jammed. He was impressed with my skills on steel, but he must have been shocked at the state of my condo. He, in fact, asked me why there were no inside doors. It was, of course, because I had kicked and smashed them in. He didn't really know that side of me that well, the destructive side. And I know he knew I was messed up from drugs. So did Mrs. Hier and Mrs. Rubin.

One time in Decarie, I phoned up a guy who fixed Gyprock. He came over to look at my apartment in the basement and said, "Yeah, this is what I do." But the magnitude of the destruction was much more than he'd expected. And he added, "I can fix it. It's what I do all the time. But it's too weird."

I got angry and was very belligerent. "Fuck off. Fuck you," I said.

And he left with no more said.

I wish I had more pictures of the wanton destruction there because words don't do the damage justice. Only what Morrie Browman said comes close. "It was Berlin 1945"—meaning there was nothing left of the city then, and my apartment was much the same.

Kenny would go there also, and we would record on Richmond. He, too, was a witness to the sheer damage. I'm sure there were no walls or doors untouched. And the noise made doing it was unbearable to the neighbors, in particular, Helen Taylor, who lived just above me and worked at night and slept during the day—when the heavy work of repairing the walls would occur. I would kick the walls with great anger and force. The plaster was thick, so it took a lot of that to break them. Raymond would come two or three times a week and take apart the walls and replace the plaster and Gyprock, but that would make a lot of noise itself, not to mention create a lot of dust. Jerry who I have on film in my place on Richmond, was another witness to the extreme damage and extent of the smashed doors, windows, walls, and contents.

I was robbed three times in succession on Decarie. As I described earlier, my front door would be kicked in and the frame broken. But nobody would find the noise out of place because of all the noise I would make on a regular basis. The first time this happened, a wad of cash that was the rent money I'd collected was taken. During subsequent break-ins, the thieves went to great lengths to try and uncover more cash, but they found none. They even slit open my punching bag in their efforts to find cash. That punching never did the good it was intended for, as all I wanted or tried to do was break the bag and smash the moorings. The other times the thieves broke in, they stole a camera so new I hadn't even developed the film yet. A second camera was later stolen too. They took three Martin guitars, two or three amps, and an ES-345—all choice stuff. The only satisfaction I had was that the Larrivée and Martins were damaged when I finished with them and were, therefore, not as valuable as they could have been.

I'll discuss my dreams now. I dreamt last night about Jerry. He was a skilled worker, and he set up a type of electrical installation. There were peppers in charge from some French newspaper, and I was pretending to be asleep but was really peeking out from mostly closed eyes while feigning sleep. Jerry had skills and was able to do work by hand. He was adept at what he was doing, which was what he had actually learned in school. In reality, Jerry had no such skills. But the emphasis was he was only setting up a thing with wires within his scope. Still, I was impressed with what he was able to do. He knew what he was doing.

Later on, I was on Alpine trying to replace a bulb in the closet down in the basement. But I had a little mini bulb when what I needed was a full-size bulb. I had to connect the string that you pulled to activate the light. I think I was able to do it. The bulb was tiny, but it worked once I had connected the clip that was attached to the string. My father was nearby, so I couldn't break anything but had to fix the light, which I did.

So, I dreamt about Jerry and my father once more, as I usually did. I never moved on from Alpine and Jerry as my best friend. This was recently. I think my mother was not around. She may even have been dead, although she far outlived my father—by more than twenty years. But I never lived on Alpine after my father died. In fact, I hadn't been there for a while before he was gone.

The work Jerry learned surprised me. I didn't know Jerry had such skills with his hands. He was working in conjunction with a friend/boss at an important and powerful company, and he seemed to be getting well paid for his work, which was good work. But the French bosses came around while I was feigning sleep, and things were changing. They may have no longer wanted Jerry or his work. Jerry was working with a spool of wire. My father was not mad at me, as I was fixing something, not breaking it. Even still, the fixing and repairing was not exactly right or properly repaired. It was fixed but not fully or fixed with a full-size bulb. But the string with a clip was attached to the fixture and it, in fact, worked. My father seemed to be worried about what was actually happening in real life. He was afraid I would be destroying something, as opposed to doing what Jerry was doing, which was good, skilled work. It seemed his law school or lawyer skills were transferred to a practical domain.

My mother, in all the dreams, was a woman with lots of power that she sometimes wielded negatively and someone who was out of control. Or maybe she was in control, as she was definitely in control of me. She had frightening control and was usually sick or crazy. This made me feel scared. She was usually in control of much more than she was in real life. And in real life, she was a terror and dictated a lot when it came to people's life in a negative way!

My mother impacted almost everybody in a bad or negative way. There was maybe an exception when it came to her friends, like Kate and Elsa and Queenie. But she fixed Queenie up with Morris and they got married, and it didn't work out too well. The marriage was the first for Morris. And it would be like me if I got married for the first time at fifty-eight after having been a bachelor for thirty-five years. He was a hypochondriac and needed constant care and attention from Queenie. Anyway, my mother had them both over for supper, and I guess they hit it off because they soon were married. Elsa Helen and Armand and Kate all liked Mom and accepted her as she was. To live with my mother was to be caught under her crazy spell. But to see her every now and then, especially with company, was much easier. Her friends understood her and accepted her, and she was always sweet with them, even when she was on the warpath with one of the family or the whole family. I found her friends soothed her and calmed her down, and she would take a sweet tone of voice with them. I always liked when they would visit and come for supper and looking back now treasured these company visits. I was always very sociable and loved to come down from my bedroom and talk to them. I also liked Lou and Bea and we would always have some beer to offer Lou. Even Gil was nice, and he would sing and be very impressive. My mother was definitely on her best behavior with the company. Some would call her a hypocrite, but I saw it as time out from her cages. Whatever the case, I never once saw her as volatile with her friends.

I also loved it on Friday afternoons, when Zaida would sometimes come for the weekend from Ottawa by train. I loved him and enjoyed and looked forward to his visits. I was very much my father's son and would sit in the den with the company and listen to the dialogue. But I was very attached to my father, and I felt he looked after me and protected me. Even now when I look back on these days, I have very fond memories. But that is not to say the times were actually that good.

I got into a fight with Dorreen, my therapist, on Thursday. I made noise outside her office, and she accused me, or so I thought, of doing it intentionally. I got mad, as if she was criticizing me or picking on me, which made me irate. I took it personally, and we fought for about the first ten minutes at the appointment. She was trying to tell me she was not criticizing me, only pointing something out. But I felt victimized, which is a part of the past I dislike visiting, a flash from the past that has very negative feelings. Anyway, with Dorreen, I felt almost like I was having a fight with a girlfriend and then, unbelievably, I felt like making up sexually. It was the time I'd felt that way with Dorreen. I felt like having sex to make up, which was ludicrous. I don't know why I saw her in that light, but it actually felt like we were having a quarrel—the type I used to have with girls I went out with when I felt persecuted, which is a very dangerous feeling. In the past, I might have gotten physically violent; but it was even more likely that I'd feel greatly offended. That's what this argument felt like. In addition, Dorreen seemed a great deal more feminine than she usually seemed—very out of character and out of place and foreign these days. But unlike a lover's fight from twenty years ago, I probably made even more noise when I got outside when the apartment was over. It felt really strange, but I didn't mention any of this to Dorreen. Maybe my reaction was because I got close to Laura, and sex was really good with her. There was also Diane and getting close and seeing her, and maybe that's why sex was interjected into the mix with Dorreen. It wasn't a good or comfortable feeling this "sexual healing." But I'm sure it was related to Laura's visit to my house on Monday late afternoon and evening. Whatever the case, it threw me for a loop and had a huge effect on me.

Dorreen said that my making more noise and our subsequent fight was, at least partially, because of my feelings for Diane and our getting closer, at least in my mind. So, between Laura and Diane, there was sex, affection, and maybe even love. The time with Laura was very intense, and I think I actually, for a while, saw her as a potential relationship or girlfriend. We talked about going swimming together and even doing something on New Year's Eve. There was more passion between us, and we necked, which is not something Laura usually permits. Our connection was emotional, beyond just having sex and paying for it, which I always do with Laura. And Diane and her daughter Joanna, both of whom I like, cleaned my house, along with the Monday hotels. We went to the Cirque du Soleil on the Wednesday afternoon the day before my appointment with Dorreen.

So, in summary, my difficult period involved breaking everything on Decarie, along with floors in other buildings and whatever I could get my hands on in apartments 1 and 6 of dad's buildings. I kicked and smashed glass business doors on Decarie. I ruined the entire condo—there were no cupboard or doors left. The downstairs neighbor had to move because of noise. They sued me. I broke urinal pipes at the country bar, resulting in a flood. I broke ten windshields in several cars over time. I drove back from Cape Cod with a broken window. I was told could rave in at any time. I broke other cars windshields—maybe five times.

So, with all of this, these scary emotions came out at my apartment on Thursday morning, half an hour later than our usual time. So, Diane is the future maybe, and Laura is wanton sex, and Dorreen gets into my head. It's a funny but powerful combination. I hope this coming Thursday is more stable. But I felt attacked by Dorreen's comments. She says all the things that are happening are the reason I'm more nervous and making more noise, which is probably true.

A wasted time in my life was when I was trying to move on Cranbrooke in CSL. I was continually walking back and forth and practicing extreme rituals on very hot days. It would take ten minutes to carry something next door.

I left two birds with no food or water for one week to go traveling. They were almost dead when I came back.

Leading up to all this, at fourteen or so, Jerry and I became very close. We played music together, and one winter in high school, we went to Sutton to ski. Another time in 1969, we went to the Newport folk festival. Most of these excursions and adventures were his idea. After that, we grew our hair long and discovered hash, grass, and acid. We both went to Sir George and, after a year of wanton drug taking, rented a pad on Overdale that was the real beginning of my problems. I felt lost and panicked on one mescaline trip. I was alone, as I usually was.

Sometime in the 1980s, there were a group of guys I would jam with—younger college students. And we would play and get drunk and have fun. One night when we were drinking a lot, I kept going upstairs to the kitchen to get more beer. But each time I took drinking glasses out of the cupboard, I would bite down on them with my teeth. I cracked maybe eight glasses in this way. And my fingers were all bandaged up from pulling the glasses apart. With these guys, I used to have fun and play at frat parties. Another time earlier in the mid-1970s, a friend of a friend came to Montreal from Boston to visit me at Alpine, my parents' house. Lori stayed in the guest room downstairs, and my mother thoroughly embarrassed me by kicking her out of the house. My out-of-control mother said, "You're leaving here and not staying another day."

Lori was shocked, and her visit was blemished. Just like Barbara, my girlfriend, a couple of years before, she was thrown out. Barbara, who I lost my virginity to, was horrified by my mother's behavior, which was completely unwarranted. But now I lead a largely normal life compared to this story. So ends my totally irregular history.

Printed in the United States
by Baker & Taylor Publisher Services